# Angel Messages from the Heart Nebula

# By the Same Author

*Spiritual Reality: Transforming the
Ordinary into the Extraordinary*

# *Angel Messages from the Heart Nebula*

## Supporting Us and the Earth

# Lydia Anne Mitchell Ph.D.

Joyful Earth
Publishing

Published in 2021 by Joyful Earth Publishing



ISBN Paperback: 979-8-9853433-0-4
Ebook: 979-8-9853433-1-1



Disclaimer
The intent of the author is only to offer information of a general nature
to help you in your quest for emotional and spiritual wellbeing. In the
event you use any of the information in this book for yourself, the
author and the publisher assume no responsibility for your actions.

A CIP catalogue copy of this book can be
found in the British Library.

Published with the help of Indie Authors World
www.indieauthorsworld.com

This book is dedicated to Mother Earth, our home,
our sustenance, and a part of us.

# Acknowledgements

To my lifelong and patient guides who have helped me on all levels, from shopping to confidence in my spiritual discoveries.

To my new angels who are taking me a step further in discovery: Angie, George, Frederica, and Newton.

I would also like to thank all the people and friends in my life who have supported me personally on many levels, my supportive husband, and all those wonderful professionals and authors I have had the pleasure of working with, and reading.

You have all added to my life more than I can say. I am truly blessed.

# Contents

# Preface

We are living in a world of creations. Some are obviously ours; some we are reluctant to acknowledge. When you start a physical project, you have an intention for that project. Without the intention, you would not start the project. In a similar way, whatever we do in life we first have an intention, a desire to go in a certain direction. Our intentions are associated with feelings and thoughts. These are often subconscious and programmed by our history and surroundings.

Throughout this book and my previous book, I mention the phrase *for the good of all*. In other words, what I create and encourage others to create *is for the good of all.* This includes you!

This, for me, is not a catchphrase, but a serious request of the Universal God. It ensures that everything created is something that not only serves me but fits in with and serves others that I know nothing about. There is a large world out there and I am not privy to, nor try to be privy to, it all. So, the solution for me is to ask God to take care of the details for me.

Another reason I use this phrase is as insurance that no energies destructive to the goal of raising our frequency and that of the Earth are permitted to enter into the equation of these goals.

I first used it with surprising effectiveness over 20 years ago. I had visited friends, and some strangers were present that made me uncomfortable. Afterwards, I had a long hour-drive home in the dark on a lonely country road in the middle of Iowa. I started to *think* things that were not very pleasant. Suddenly it occurred to me that it was not me doing the *thinking*. To test this out, I stated in my mind very clearly with intention *If you are not for the good of all – leave now*. The negative thoughts just vanished, and I had a sense of lightness. The negative energies had to leave, as I had not given them permission to be in my space.

This is a very important Universal Law. What we do not agree with in our space is not permitted in our space. You might say that you do not agree with some things that happen, or people that enter your space. They enter your space because there is a need in some form for them to be there; some lesson that you, on a soul level, are learning. If you truly do not want them there, you need to be clear in your mind as well as clear on the vacuum that their absence will create.

Mind you, it may take longer for a physical being to leave than a nonphysical being that can leave instantaneously.

Having a question or prayer of inspiration in your mind is a good focus to hold while reading these pages, to find what you need with ease. It is always fun, I think, to just open the book at any page and see what you are guided to at the time. It is rather like pulling divination cards, and it never fails.

I would, though, like you to keep in mind that you are the author of your story. You are capable and strong, as well as adaptable and caring. Know that it will always be your story to create. However, you do not need to face all of your challenges alone. Others are here to help in many forms, on Earth and in the heavens – there is a universe of others to help you, if only you ask.

The words in this book are a form of energy. The words come from thought to form to you, and your mind. Let them flow, shift, and strengthen you in love.

# Introduction

I wrote this book to add to the information of understanding, clarity, and development in this changing period.

This book is basically about the frequencies that make up your lives.

What do I mean by frequency? Think of a wave pattern – oscillating waves. They have an infinite variety of forms. The amplitude can change – or how high the wave goes. The frequency is how many waves you can get in one unit – be it a box, or the Universe. Then there is the combination of waves where they create new patterns as they combine, like multiple ripples in a lake when stones are thrown in one after the other. There are infinite possibilities, just as there are infinite forms of existence. Each of us is a new and unique version of the human species. We have an infinite variation and variety.

You are made up of atoms in the solid state. But in reality, you are not very solid. Even your atoms have huge spaces between the components in what makes up your cells. It is also where frequencies come in. Your atoms are oscillating at specific frequencies. These were the frequencies that I measured as a research chemist when identifying the structure and composition of organic compounds. I put samples in a super conducting magnet and irradiated them with radio frequencies which flipped the energy levels in the atoms. This enabled me to measure their specific and identifying frequencies.

The water in your body changes its vibrational frequency when it is in different organs. This is how MRI scans work – they map out the corresponding frequencies of the water atoms found in different locations of the body.

My first book, *Spiritual Reality*, is about awakening spirituality and describes my experiences over the last 30 years, telepathically connecting with my guides to obtain answers to my personal questions, as well as using muscle testing and dowsing. I have since started to communicate telepathically with entities from the Heart Nebula, which resulted in this book. It is a downloaded book, if you will.

Let's get back to frequencies outside of the body. Those frequencies that you use daily to communicate on the phone, watch television, listen to songs on the radio. The internet is another wonderful example of free-floating frequencies that come to your home and are translated by electronics to give you a message you can understand. You cannot see these with the human eye – yet they are accepted as part of your daily life. We have been trained as a society to be quite comfortable with these frequencies being invisible.

There are other frequencies that we are surrounded by which are not deciphered by electronic equipment. To decipher or receive them, we need to be in a state of mind that is open to these frequencies and also open to receiving them. We need to be of a frequency that can match and connect with other unseen frequencies. Our bodies are electromagnetic beings that can interact with other frequencies. Evidence of this is an electrocardiogram (ECG or EKG) and sensitivity around electromagnetic frequencies (EMF) generated by electronics that interact with our body. These have been found to affect the immune system of sensitive individuals over time and create health issues for them. In general, we have not learned to respect the less physical aspect of our bodies, like electric impulses – even though it is what makes our nervous system run and our bodies work. Without this electro-magnetic system, our brain, muscles, and immune system would not work. We are a truly wonderful and complex arrangement of atoms.

We all have the ability to connect with other frequencies, depending on our own frequency level. Each level we are at is important and part of our growth. You would not want a toddler to cook dinner; it would be dangerous for the toddler as well as the stove. In a similar way, we would not want to have access to frequencies that would overwhelm our current comfort zone and state of knowledge.

This book is about conversations I have had with four 'angels'. I call them angels because they are nonphysical beings of a different frequency to those of us currently in these wonderful bodies. You can call them spirits or higher frequencies (since they are not in the physical form), or whatever you choose. I have decided that I like to call them angels. To me, it embodies the concept of beings that are benevolent, loving, supportive, and understanding.

We tend to assume that those with a more distant perspective have more insight and knowledge than we are able to gain in this physical form. The view of most things changes with perspective when seen from a distance. The Heart Nebula is indeed very distant – 7,500 light years (a light year is the distance light travels in a year) or 9,460,730,472,581 kilometers away. These angels that I am connecting with come from this region, in the sense that they spend a great deal of the time in the Heart Nebula.

I was guided to write this book for quite a while, but I hesitated through fear and uncertainty. However, in the end I decided to just ask questions of these angels and see where it led. After all, life is to be lived and experienced. Without curiosity, where would be the fun and knowledge gained? I hope that you also find food for thought in these questions and answers.

The format of the book is to talk to one angel at a time and ask questions of them. The overall goal I have in doing this is for the good of all. I intend that these words will help both the people who read them as well as the planet that supports us in this amazing physical universe.

The names I have for these angels came to me telepathically, as did their answers.

The first angel is called Angie – she likes this name, and it is a bit like an angel in concept. I *see* her as tall and in green.

I hope that you enjoy and gain some insights from these conversations as much as I have enjoyed writing them.

# CHAPTER 1

# Angie´s Answers
# on the Changing Earth

**Question:**

Hello, Angie. Is Angie your real name?

**Answer:**

No, but it is a nice name, and you like it. It is as good as any other name that you and others will relate to.

**Question:**

Why are you interacting with me?

**Answer:**

There are many people on the planet who are growing curious about the other realms of existence. Not in a religious sense that has been organised and defined for many groups. People want to go beyond the defined boundaries. They are becoming curious. Part of this curiosity is inevitable, with the rapid changes in the society, population growth, and planetary changes.

There are many answers to the questions people ask in the media and internet – almost as many answers as questions. This in itself can be confusing, and even discouraging, if one wants a definite answer. So often, what is definite for one person is not for another – hence the many options that are available.

We simply want to give another positive option. Something that some people can relate to while others may not, information that makes sense to people. It will help them to come to grips with both themselves and their changing world. We hope to add some positive and beneficial thoughts and encouragement to those who resonate with our message.

There are so many wonderful books and messages being poured onto the planet. These are here to give balance to a rapidly changing world. You have so much information – positive, and sometimes discouraging, which plays a part in creating your reality on the Earth.

I am also going to communicate the needs and feelings of the Earth at this time of change. Coming from the Heart Nebula, I have much empathy for the changes happening. The Heart Nebula is itself always in change – it is the norm of creation. Here, the Earth has been quiet for some time, and so you are not used to the concept of dramatic change. You do not know how to adapt.

I would like to help you with the adaption. I do this both for you and the planet.

**Question:**

What are the changes to the Earth that you are talking about?

**Answer:**

There has been much talk about the transition into the 5th dimension. This in part is true. There are those who will be going willingly and happily into the 5th dimension. Through love and joy, they will be united with others in that frequency. This does not make them any better or 'higher' than those that choose otherwise. Those that have experiences they would still like to experience in a 3rd dimensional reality can do so on one of the millions of options available. Your scientists estimate that there are between 30 and 70 billion trillion stars in the Universe.

There are thought to be 6 billion Earth-like stars in the Milky Way alone.

The Earth itself is heading for the 7th dimension. How can a planet be in the 7th Dimension, you ask? In much the same way as the Heart Nebula is there and not there. Its physical form has dispersed to be created and recreated. This is not an issue for those beings at a similar frequency who do not have the solidness that you experience here.

But do not fear. This will not happen overnight; it is a progression, as most things are. First the Earth wants to guide its children in the gentleness of transitions. Those interested in this shift can progress with the Earth.

**Question:**

How can people progress with the Earth?

**Answer:**

They would need to defocus from the current negative feed of news media and negative belief systems. These are being fed into the planet as a means of control to keep the status quo.

This means focusing on positive news and news which promotes the community supporting each other, as well as valuing each other. It involves seeing the individuals as your children in a way – beings that you value and take care of in whatever way that you can.

It means letting go of much of your ego conversation – including the 'spiritual' ego which says your religion or spiritual belief is the correct one for all. Each belief has its place and need for individuals who follow it.

It is like having different flowers in a garden. It would be very boring for you if they were all the same. Similarly, each of us is an individual, and we attract and need specific ideas and support for our particular situation.

It is important to respect your individuality. This does not mean that you condone the actions of those that are cruel, deceptive, egotistical, and destructive. These are traits that will disappear when not fed by your focus. The more you focus on these situations with judgement and fear, the more you are feeding them with your negative energy.

The more they grow, and you diminish. It is like the negative news and violent movies – they draw you out and create fear, which creates more fear.

Being aware of what you want to create in these low energy situations is important in shifting the energy to a higher frequency.

The more grounded you are in your own goals and frequency, the more effective you are in manifesting your desires for a happy and peaceful world.

Judgement, fear, and criticism reduce your focus. Start to focus on what you want. There are many options now on the internet, and books as well as courses. Take some time to think of how you want to shift your focus and onto what you want to shift it. Start creating your realities in a more focused way.

Then enjoy the fruits of your choices.

**Question:**

What dimension are you from?

**Answer:**

The word dimension is an Earth term to designate levels. They are visualised as going up into the skies. In fact, there are no levels going up into the skies.

There are just different frequencies which vibrate at different rates and produce different results. It is natural for you to feel there is something better out there and that you are in the lower levels.

As a species, you are always wonderfully striving. It is part of your characteristics to seek to 'better' yourself. The concept that you are already 'better' does not come into play unless you have started to see the bigger picture of frequencies with all their options.

You are another option and as such are perfect, even in your assumed imperfection, which is striving for perfection.

So, to answer your question, in your terms I would be considered from the 11th dimension.

**Question:**

How many dimensions are there?

**Answer:**

It is not so much that there are levels of dimensions. Even though you give them numbers – as I mentioned earlier – it is another frequency. The numbers are convenient for the different ranges of frequencies.

In fact, if you want to know how many levels there are, there is an infinite number of levels. There is always creation and multiples of creation. Some are parallel and some are in layers. They are all groupings of creation.

**Question:**

How old are you?

**Answer:**

As old as you are. I am just in another form and dimension of experience. We are all one. That is why it is so odd at times that you fight and believe that what you do to hurt others does not hurt yourself. I have chosen this path right now. I have also been in bodies – not on your Earth, but there are many choices. You have chosen this Earth, and a wonderful mother to you she is.

Be glad for whatever befalls you here, for it is all of your choosing and for your benefit. You are not judged by others when you are done here. You are the master of your creations and will decide what you want to do next.

Yes, from your viewpoint you cannot jump classes, so to speak. From 3rd to 11th dimension without amazing changes, it would be unlikely and undesirable from your point of view. On the other hand, you could go from 11th to 3rd dimension, as it is reducing density and frequency. If you felt there was a reason and it was to your liking, you would be able to reduce your density. You could want some special experience in the body of the 3rd dimension and make an agreement to go to that dimension.

Or you could choose to help in some other way – as I am doing. There are many Earth telepaths who are willing and able to communicate with us and be grounded in the Earth energy to transmit the information that can support the growth of the people and the planet.

The idea of age is very Earth-related. Time is split up, but in fact it is simultaneous and ever-present. However, linear timelines are convenient for the day-to-day running of your offices and lives – it gives you a measure. Measures are very much appreciated in your society. You, like me, are infinite souls acting out a path that you created to enjoy another experience and learn along the way.

There are so many options that you have on this world: race, colour, finances, family, friends, career, country, sex, and religion. There are infinite choices to be born into. If you wanted another option, there is always another life to try.

We were all created at the same time the God that is did in fact split himself/herself to many parts to create an infinite variety of planets and beings. These in turn forgot that they belonged to the body of the infinite God, as it should be in order to create diversity and life at infinitum.

**Question:**

Why is time so important for us?

**Answer:**

It gives you a sense of accomplishment that you have a defined space in which to do something, and you can feel you have accomplished what you set out to do within certain parameters.

Time gives you a framework to measure your lives by. It gives you a sense of movement. Going from one year to the next, you are reminded that there are only so many years left. This makes you more conscious of what you are doing and if it is worthwhile.

If you were clear on being an infinite being in infinite time, none of these consequences would show themselves.

In other words, time behaves as a sort of consequence to your actions. You grow old, you grow sick, and want to take better care of your bodies. Without this sense of time, you would feel ever-young and invincible – with the consequence you would not need to learn how to look after your lovely bodies or heal yourself or the Earth. It would all be invisible to you.

So, time in fact is your teacher and friend. It was constructed to be so. Just as you were constructed to be born into little bodies and then grow into little people, and then finally grow into the adult form of you.

Time helps to keep you in the illusion of separation. You measure things by time and so do not look at the frequencies involved. It helps keep you in the physical world, in the here and now.

You say, well, there is history. Yes, but even history depends on the historian. At a frequency level, books can be changed, records disappear, and memories fade. So, in fact although reference is made to past centuries, they have little meaning to most people in the present.

Time is really all about the present. It is about keeping you in this reality of physical matter at this point in time. The past is non-existent other than in your memory or cellular absorption of the events (usually traumatic). The future is yet to be created by you and those in your story of life. Other than fear of the future, it does not really register with you as a real thing – just as the past does not register as a real thing.

That is why there is so much talk of living in the present – that is all there really is – and it is what the construct of time was meant to give you. The construct of time gives you a sense of responsibility for the present that you are living.

**Question:**

What is the 11$^{\text{th}}$ dimension like where you are from?

**Answer:**

I am not actually from anywhere. A frequency can be spread over vast distances measured in light years. I may concentrate more in one area than another at times – for example, I love the Heart Nebula. It is a favourite place of mine, with its changing forms and high frequency energy. I resonate to this energy. I see inter-dimensional space via the frequencies that exist. I follow those as one would follow a river.

**Question:**

What are your goals in talking to me?

**Answer:**

I too have taken on goals, as you have on your Earth. My goals tend to be of a form that increase the surrounding frequencies. Talking to you is doing that. It gives it a higher musical range, so to speak.

At this point in time, I am talking to you in order to help people realise that:

They are wonderful.

1. They can help the Earth shift to its assigned destiny (it assigned the destiny – just as you assigned yours);

2. To help with the choices people make during the Earth transitions, when times will be transitory;

3. And to visualise and create a wonderful 5th dimensional Earth.

The Earth will survive – it always has, even given some rather destructive human activity.

However, it would also be nice if as many as possible of the souls of various forms also survived into the new dimension. For as many souls to survive, there needs to be a pulling together of people uniting for the good of all.

# CHAPTER 2

# George's Answers
# on Helping Mother Earth

I see George as short, with whitish skin.

**Question:**

Hello, George. Please tell us about yourself, and why you have chosen to communicate.

**Answer:**

Well, as you already know, I am a talker so would be happy to enlighten you on myself and my goals.

For the first part of your question as to who I am – I am what you call a spirit or angel. I am a non-physical being who would like to connect with you as a physical being for the good of all.

You have asked for help and understanding, and so we, the four of us, have come to connect with you for the goal of raising the frequency on the planet Earth.

This is not to say it is a bad frequency here – on the contrary, it is quite agreeable. However, at this time there are shifts in the mother planet that need more support from those with a different perspective. She is undergoing a birthing process of her own personal development.

You have a saying 'As above so below'. In other words, the more you as her guests develop and support her, the more she will be able to grow and develop. With the combined and unified form, it is anticipated that the process will go much smoother for all involved.

By this I mean the surface dwellers and the Mother Earth herself. Less undulations and temperature shifts which would be destructive to those above and below the planet.

**Question:**

How can we help Mother Earth and support her in these shifts?

**Answer:**

There are numerous ways – some quite straightforward, and others more esoteric, and yet others that appear to you to be quite strange.

Let us start with the straightforward ways of supporting Mother Earth. These are the physical things that require uniting and gathering together, as well as inventive ideas. But then, many of you are inventive.

1. Recycle – yes, I know you have heard it
   before, and it is almost a joke amongst
   some of you.
   Think about it – over 7.8 billion people with
   a population over double today what it was
   in 1970. That is a lot of garbage, and it is
   increasing rapidly. It only goes away if it is
   dealt with.

2. Then there is the electromagnetic overflow
   that comes with all those people. The Earth
   has grid works that are empty in
   unpopulated areas. In populated areas, the
   electric energy from the house is grounded
   with wires into the Earth. The Earth needs
   to do something with all this electrical
   energy. It puts it in the natural grids around
   the world, called Hartman and Curry Grids.
   The problem for people comes as they
   cannot avoid living and working over these
   grids. They are living over an electromagnet
   flow which subtly affects their
   electromagnetic body. It can subconsciously
   stop people from entering businesses. It can
   negatively affect the immune system over
   time. In short, the grid work is full and can
   be destructive to those living above the grid
   lines.
   There are ways to create energy,
   communicate, and systems that are not
   harmful to the Earth or the people

inhabiting it. These need to be installed and used.

3. Growing food in a way that respects Mother Earth and hence produces more crops without the chemical toxicity that also affect the 'good' as well as the 'bad' insects. You have made a start with Organic and now Biodynamic farming, however the temptation to keep those supermarkets full of perfect looking food all year round is taking its toll on the farmers and especially those that are smaller. The tendency towards larger and larger farms has led to factory farms and the subsequent loss of energy in the food. This in turn leads to weaker people and immune systems, as well as a drained Earth. Respect and gratitude for the Earth that has produced the food enhances the energy of the food and the Earth.

These three physical issues – rubbish, electromagnetic pollution, and factory farms – are draining Mother Earth, as well as those living off of her.

In order to solve these problems and the weight they put on Mother Earth, humans need to band together and make some dramatic changes. These changes are not only for their own wellbeing but also for their family, friends, and neighbours. They are changes needed for the population to continue to have a wonderful life on the surface of a wonderful planet.

**Physical activities for global health**

In order for these changes to be thought of as something worthwhile, people need to shift in several respects.

1. Realise that they need to do something in order to continue with their happy carrot lifestyle, as it has been called.

2. Shift who they are and their sense of values to give them the courage and incentive to make and support changes.

3. Work and band together in groups, small or large, for the greater good, for the future of the lifestyle you are accustomed to ☺. Let ego fade in favour of the ultimate goal of the group – whichever one you choose to support, in whatever way you are comfortable with.
   This does not mean suffering for the greater good – if you are suffering and miserable, you will bring suffering and misery to the table. Do what you can within your timeline and comfort zone. Use the talents that you have, even if it is only putting flyers in letterboxes for half an hour.

4. The controlling structure of society needs to be in alignment with these ideas and be

willing to shift their financial focus for the good of all. This would include their own families to be in alignment with the physical changes that need to be developed for Mother Earth to continue to support humankind.

These are the grassroot levels that will ultimately shift the way people think and hence the way that politicians behave.

The next phase is the power structure which needs to shift, as basically they are in control of the world as it now stands. There is no incentive in their terms to do anything differently; they have created the situation as it stands and would be uncomfortable shifting gears, given that their egos and finances are heavily involved.

How to solve this problem?

**Frequency exercises for global health**

The peaceful and most successful way begins with an energetic approach. There are many ways to do this. I will list a few, and you can see which ones grab you.

The first step is to release aggression, fear, and anger associated with the leaders you are about to focus on. Imagine them as white knights, if you will. Detach yourself from the media presentations and all the nasty things you hear about them. Remember the white knight.

- Sit down for five minutes a day and visualise a particular leader, or leaders of a whole country. See them shifting gears to a positive approach in managing the country or arena that they control.

- Feel the shift in the country.

- Rejoice in the shift.

- Let it go.

- Go about your business

Do not think about it any more – this is important, because you can negate all the good work that you have done by self-doubt, expectations, and fear of looking silly. Though since no-one knows you are doing this, it is hard to look silly.

- When you are walking to work, or in the park, or playing with your dog or children or grandchildren – you get the idea. In those moments when you are relaxed and in joy, use the time to send some thoughts or colours. Send them to leaders who may need this energy to strengthen them, and hold them in the light of God and what is for the good of all.

- It does not have to be a specific leader – it could just be a leader who will influence a specific issue. Think of the issue and ask what colour the leader needs – a leader you may or may not know, who has power in this situation. Take whatever colour you are given and send it to this leader with faith that it will go to the right person and be the supporting frequency or colour (as all colours are specific frequencies).

- On the other hand, you may know of a specific leader who will influence something that you feel is important for the good of all. Think of that leader helping the situation and see what colour/frequency comes down from the heavens to envelop them while they are doing this wonderful thing. Focus for moments on that colour streaming down onto them, and then them smiling in acceptance.

Do these exercises whenever you think of them – hopefully once or twice a day. The more you do them, the easier it becomes when you stay in faith and joy.

They may only take a minute to do, or five minutes if you are doing the meditation.

You can also do them before you get out of bed in the morning, or last thing at night.

The main thing is to let go of expectations, do it with a joyful heart, and know that on some level you are helping the world.

These are exercises anybody can do. Joining a physical group to support a cause is also good.

Whether it is physical or energetic, the support is always welcomed by Mother Earth.

In other words, do what you can, and the energy on the planet will shift to one of construction rather than destruction. There are many of you: each one of you is a light; each one of you has your own frequency; each one of you counts at whatever you are doing and whatever levels you are at.

Each of you is a blessing. It has come a time for you to start blessing.

**Another arena to help yourself and Mother Earth.**

Many of you have been focused on creating a better life for yourself in a spiritual and physical sense. Some have focused more on the physical, and some more on the spiritual. Since you are embodied, they are both important aspects of your being. It is not fun with a body that does not do well, has much pain, and feels restricted.

On the other hand, if you focus all your energies on comfort – which, by the way, is always over the other hill – then the spiritual aspects and appreciation that give you joy can be missing. This in turn leads to a life that can be easily influenced by the temptation of material gain over the wellbeing of those around you. That is how the choices are often viewed in your society. There is a sense of lack, so that if you gain something it must be at the expense of others. This leads to much sadness for all concerned – including the one who 'gains'. They have acquired the material gain but then lack the security of the soul and often mistrust those around them, so they are never secure, either mentally or physically. It is quite a Catch 22 when you believe in a scarce universe.

When you realise that there is always more that can be created, you are free to help others and interact with them in a way that benefits you both. The soul is smiling.

This is the most efficient way for you to be – with a smiling soul.

Whatever physical gains you acquire, you can enjoy without fear, for at the bottom of it all you know that you are a soul beyond this arena – and nothing can take that away from you. So, you have the freedom to be and do for yourself, the society, and others. You can enjoy the physical as well as the frustrations and challenges involved. They are all a pathway for your soul.

This viewpoint is a wonderful one to help you through the times of trouble, as well as the times of joy. It helps you see that helping others and the Earth is a wonderful goal, which also helps you. You will see that when you have reached this place, you will be very innovative. Messages from the Universe will pop into your head to help solve the challenges you come up against. You ask for and you will receive the information that you need.

Now this is what the Earth needs, and this is what people need now. It does not mean that you are perfect – there is no such thing. By whose standards would you be perfect – a high school teacher, a friend, a parent, the newspapers? You can forget being perfect – you are what you are, and you are doing what you do to the best of your ability.

So, I am not talking about being some perfect meditating being who levitates and manifests gold spoons.

I am talking about being aware that you have a soul and helping it to smile. You do this by following your inner guidance and your sense of right and wrong. Not all sense of right and wrong comes from society. There is an innate sense in the heart of you that generally does not want to hurt others.

You have many challenges on many levels. You also have the ability to deal with them all. When there is no overall goal other than a material one, you tend to get bogged down. The mind keeps the worry buffer full of unimportant things, which really are not very satisfying for you. Hence, you have a sense of unease and are rudderless, holding onto the next thing or idea that comes to mind.

When you have a positive, uplifting goal – say, saving the world like the heroes in the movies – you actually have fewer problems. All the details in the worry buffer have been replaced by an important and big goal. Your life takes on more meaning and your soul smiles.

Now, this does not mean you don a cape and fly from buildings. It means that whatever talents you have you use for the greater good – at least, for part of the time – as say extracurricular activities. You may be good at computers, at writing, at marketing, at speaking, at filing. Saving the world requires a lot of job skills. For example, who did the sewing for that cape of Superman? Who made the thread? Who made the shoes? We all have a place in this life. If we listen to our souls and what brings us joy, we find the place where we can be of use.

Then our worry buffer shrinks, and we focus on what is important to us and, ultimately, Mother Earth.

So, this is a call to be the best you can be with the goal of helping those around you, including the land that you live on. The Earth is calling because she needs your support. In fact, the reality is that you need her support, and it is you that is in danger, not the Earth. She has wonderful ways of cleaning herself from plagues and negative energy.

However, I would like to see you work with her so that humanity can shift with the changes in the Earth. I see a society that functions on the Earth at a higher frequency and awareness; a society with the ability to look after each other with joy, respect, faith, and trust.

# CHAPTER 3

# Frederica's Answers
# on Coming From the Heart

I see Frederica like a red/rose-coloured flower, the shape of a Gerber daisy.

**Question:**

How do you fit into this group from the Heart Nebula?

**Answer:**

In some ways, I really do not fit in.

I come from the Heart Nebula a great deal of the time, but for me it is simply a portal. There is a very large doorway there – it looks rather like a spiraling whirly or tornado.

It takes you to my home, which is many light years distant. However, I use this passageway through the Heart Nebula to access other dimensions and frequencies. I have been invited to join the group because I speak very much from the heart. There is a softness and certainty in the heart which is not found in other parts of the body or places.

The heart, as you have rightly been told, is the doorway to heaven – or what you would call heaven. It is a place where troubles dissolve and you become still. You become one with all that is. In this place, there is clarity.

It is a goal that many of you have, and some have attained. It is not for all parts of the Universe to have this goal – where would be the fun and exploration in that? But it is a part of them all. It is a very important part of them, as it gives a sense of balance, and with this balance freedom.

However, it is freedom that needs to be earned so that it can be valued and used.

**Question:**

Why are you in this group?

**Answer:**

I am here to encourage you to speak from your heart. The heart you have is the master organ of your body, as well as your spirit. When you go into your heart, in the stillness you will learn the answers to many things.

When you want to adjust your chakras and balance them, you can do this by going into your heart. When your heart chakra is blocked, the energy to the others is also blocked to varying degrees. This is why emotional hurts run so deep. Emotional hurts affect the heart chakra, which then affects the rest of the body chakra systems.

It is good to learn the processes of forgiveness and understanding, and of what drives you in this life. Forgiveness especially will open the heart chakra. In order to forgive, you need to let go. When you let go, you are freeing yourself.

The trick is not to get caught and side-tracked in the analysis and feelings. When you mull over things for too long, you lose track of what really matters. You start to lose track of yourself and focus so much on your hurts and what others have done or not done. In this way, you can lose yourself and the reason you first started the search.

Do not lose track of the goal – which is to speak from the heart.

When I ask you to speak from the heart, know that you have this ability and are focused on developing the ability at this time.

I am here to remind and reinforce this concept to you. At times it may not seem possible for you. Know that it is. Ask for the ability to enter your heart, ask for your heart to expand to the level it can.

There are wonderful courses on this now. There will be more. Take advantage of those courses that call to you and support you.

**Question:**

What advice do you have for us at this time?

**Answer:**

In a sentence, follow your heart.

This is, of course, the simple version. It is always good to know what we want to do and where we want to go, to have a goal.

Why do I recommend following your heart to be a goal?

- At this time of change in your world, it is good to have an anchor. The heart energy is connected to source and so will help you through these times of transition.

- The activated heart energy will raise your own energy and be compatible with the raising energy of the Earth.

- Think of a small human, as in a child playing with enthusiasm with all the Earth has to offer, by the sea in the waves. Think of a child that is loved and safe, taught but not extensively controlled. This picture warms your heart, it gives you joy.

- When you come from the heart, you come from a sense of joy and love.

- Then, of course, it just feels good when you get the hang of it.

**Question:**

How best can we approach coming from our heart?

**Answer:**

- Set an intention to come from the heart for at least part of a day. It could be for as little as five minutes.

- Ask the divine to help you in a gentle and kind way that you can assimilate.

- Attend classes that resonate with you, where you feel safe, and the people are authentically working for the good of all.

- Feel joy as much and as often as you can, for as little reason as you can. Laugh at a seagull, smile at a flower, bark with a dog if it makes you smile (when people are not looking).

- Meditate on your heart chakra and smile at it often. Do five breaths through your nose in and out, while mentally smiling at your heart area and chakra.

**A Heart Chakra Meditation:**

To go into your heart, think of your physical heart area. Not the exact physical heart, but the area it is in within the body. Imagine it as a vast ocean, and hear the waves softly crashing onto shore.

It is powerful, it is gentle, and it nourishes life.

It does not take sides or judge.

It is infinite.

Feel yourself as part of this infinite and timeless ocean. Then smile internally and take a little bit of it with you wherever you go.

Come from this limitless place, even if only for moments at a time. You are coming from the heart as you see it. When you do this meditation, images may come to you that feel positive and in alignment with what you think of as your heart. You can incorporate these images into your meditations.

**Question:**

When you are not here, where are you?

**Answer:**

I am there ☺.

Yes, the *there* varies. Generally, I am in a non-physical dimension. The dimensions I am in carry a high vibration as a norm. Think of it as being in a wonderful group of people who you may know. They have the same values of respect, truth, love, and joy. They are peaceful in their lives and in the resolution of issues that arise for them. They are generally honest with themselves and the society or group they are in. They have goals and 'work' to do. They are developing and creating on their own planes.

Unlike you, they do not have the physical bodies that you have chosen to work with.

Like me, they work with the physical matter of the Universe, of stars and dust clouds of black holes, and of course my favorite, the Heart Nebula.

There are billions of stars and planets in the Universe. Your galaxy alone has more than 3,200 other stars, with planets orbiting them. Your solar system is just one specific planetary system.

Then there are millions of solar systems. It can be quite a playground.

But remember that you, with your solid frequencies, have a vast playground as well. You just have not connected with all the possibilities yet. When you start accessing the spiritual or higher frequencies of yourself and your planet, your playing field will expand.

You may think that life would be boring without the drama that you are fed daily. With no arguments, illness, and disappointment to identify you and talk about, that you would be bored with so much love and joy.

You will find there are other challenges that come to light and new creations to create. The Universe is ever in motion – like the sea, it is always moving and creating. You too can create in the physical realm in an expanded way when you access your heart chakra.

The heart chakra takes you out of ego – even spiritual ego. You are still you – just an expanded and more helpful version to the Earth and those around you.

So, fear not for the changes in you or around you. Let go, and go with the flow of life. Your planet has been accelerating over the last 100 years at an exponential rate. You often forget how hard life was for mankind in the centuries past.

The faster the development, the faster you have to keep up with the changes. This can be a challenge for you.

**Question:**

How can we keep up with the rapid changes in the Earth and society?

**Answer:**

You know who you are in the world around you. Often, you are told you are this or that. Or you think you are this or that. But really, at some level you know who you are.

Take away the external view of yourself and start listening to your inner voice. Do experiments to see what the results are. For example, if you feel bad about a person and do not want to be in their energy – stay away. Do not be rude about it, just disappear. You will find that when you do not need the reflection of a particular type of person, they will disappear from your circle. This is only an example of starting to trust your inner resources and experimenting with it.

Do not judge yourself if you think you have failed at something.

There is so much judgement here – you yourselves judge, and others judge you. It puts a stop to creativity and moving forward in whatever direction you want to go.

When you start to trust yourself and your inner guidance, you will unite with others and attract them to you. This will reinforce the process of your own development. You will not be alone in your thoughts.

Then at some point, you need to intend to shift with the Earth.

Intend to shift to the 5th dimension with it. This sounds very scary to you right now, because you do not know what that looks and feels like. It is very human to stay where you are even if you are unhappy, but comfortable with knowing what it is that you have. It is a challenging step to take when you do not know where the ground is next.

Without your intention to join into the higher frequency shift, nothing will happen for you.

It is a law of the Universe. Ask and you shall receive. Do not ask and you will not receive.

Of course, the asking is again that challenging step. But really, what do you have to lose? Where are you going if you do not go with the transformed Earth? That is even a bigger challenge to answer. Your body will of course die, as it was meant to do eventually. This is something that happens to all human bodies, though often you conveniently forget this part of the arrangement.

If you do not transform your frequencies to that of the changing Earth, what will you do? What are your options? When you die, you will find another Earth so to speak, and in this sense it is fine. There are many planets and many choices. Mind you, this one is particularly fine for the physical aspects. So yes, you really do not have to *intend* to shift frequency and go to the 5th dimension with the Earth. You are an eternal soul – you will go where you will, where you experience what it is you want to experience.

There is no right or wrong – there is only choice. I am here to talk about the choices you have, which till now are not generally known.

**Question:**

What choices do we have now?

**Answer:**

Now the main choices you face, whether you know it or not, are to go with the changing flow of energy in the Earth, or to resist the changes in energy.

**Question:**

What does this mean, and how does it look?

**Answer:**

To resist the changes in energy of the Earth paradoxically means to continue in the same way that you have been living. There is more and more media pressure to focus on fear and hopelessness of the power of the individual, more focus on the material, and less on the values that would set you free of the increasing stress and fear.

When you concentrate on the restrictive frequencies sent to you in this manner, you are being confined and lessened. You lose faith in yourself and those around you. In this way you can become less powerful and more dependent on those in control. You, in turn, magnify these energies and send them to the Earth.

Basically, you are frequency transmitters. You are electromagnetic beings. This facet of your nature has been used constructively in research and medicine. You yourselves have not been taught how powerful this combination of electromagnetic frequencies and intention on your part can be.

This leads me to the second option. In this option you own your own special electromagnetic power and focus it with intention to help the planet Earth and those on board.

**Question:**

How can we focus our electromagnetic power for the greater good?

**Answer:**

- First, you have to have that as an intention. You need to decide that you want to help the greater good.

- Then you ask for divine help from sources that are more than willing to help you.

- You meet with similar minded people and help each other.

- Know that colour is a form of frequency. The advantage is that it does not have any form of attachment to it. It is pure frequency. You give it meaning with the aura colours and, yes, certain frequencies have certain effects and power. However, there is no moral in the frequencies of colour – they just are. As such, they are a wonderful healing tool.

- You let go of preconceived ideas of what you should do.

- You open yourself up to find ways to connect with the Earth – whether it is sitting on the ground or walking barefoot thanking the Earth for all it has done. Ask the Earth what you can do for it and see what answers come – if not immediately, then in time. You will know what the answers are because they feel good in your heart. You have requested this for the good of all, so you cannot go wrong!

- Start sending light to the various world leaders. Before you do this, ask your higher self to communicate with the higher selves of those leaders that are willing to receive healing light. Your higher self is the part of you that connects with God, and through

God can connect with the higher self of the other person. God is the intermediary.

- The light you send does not come with conditions other than it is for the good of all. It also does not matter who the leader is – they all need light and support from the light. When their higher selves have agreed, you can be sure that it is an agreement through God. Do not worry about what colour to send them – just whatever comes to mind for the good of all. They will get the frequencies they need from the colour sent.

- Similarly, if you feel a part of the world needs support, send that area the colour that comes to mind. You only have to do this for five or ten minutes a day to have an effect. You could be doing it in the shower or when you get your cup of coffee. There is no need to meditate and do it – unless that is what you would prefer; the main thing is to do it!

**Question:**

Are there other ways we can focus our electromagnetic power for the greater good?

**Answer:**

There are many forms of frequency. In fact, everything is made up of frequencies. The longer frequencies create dense matter; the shorter wavelengths are not visible at your frequency or the ability of your eyes – for example, UV light.

So, when you have thoughts, they are also a frequency. A frequency you send out into the Universe. This may seem like an exaggeration – but in fact it is a reality. There is nothing to stop frequencies from passing through space and matter as you see it.

An example of this you know from your feng shui work. A geopathic, as you know, is what is called negative energy from the Earth. It is of a frequency that interacts harmfully with humans and plants. Often this is the area that the Earth has channelled the excess electrical energy you send to ground in buildings and houses. The Earth contains it in the originally empty grids all over the planet. A geopathic can pass through 30 floors of a building and negatively affect the people in those floors.

So, your thoughts in fact know no bounds! This is both good news and not so good news for you.

The good news is that you can use this ability to send thought frequencies to others around the planet. The trickier news is you need to be careful what you think! You may not see the consequences immediately, but your thoughts are out in the air and beyond, ready to be received by those who can and will decipher your thoughts from the millions of others. They are usually people connected with you in some way, and hence will at some level tune into your thoughts. This is one of the reasons it is good to be as honest as you can be with yourself, and then as honest as you are able to be with others.

Back to the subject at hand of focusing your electromagnetic power for the greater good. These thoughts of yours can be used for the good of all, if you so choose. You can direct your thoughts to certain people or situations. You do this without judgement. You are simply sending positive messages to certain people, with a request to shift their actions for the good of all. It is a little bit like having a polite conversation with someone – only they are not in front of you.

When you make a thought request, it is vitally important that you do not judge the person or situation that you are connecting with. It is also important that you do not judge them or yourself if the situation does not go as you would wish. You are asking *for the good of all.*

In fact, from your perspective you can only guess what that means. Therefore, there needs to be a high level of detachment on your part. This does not mean you are emotionless or without your opinions and desires which initiated the interaction. It means that you give those emotions up for moments at a time to a higher perspective and have trust and faith that what is happening is for the highest good for all.

**Question?**

What are the steps in the process of sending mental requests?

**Answer:**

You are the main step ☺ Here is a recommended sequence to use:

- First and foremost, you need to be clear on your intention. It needs to be something that you wish for with emotion, and that you do consider for the good of all. Not something that is mainly motivated to give you or your friends financial gain, or to be used primarily to gain attention for your egos.

- Next, reserve judgement on the acts and outcome, leaving it to the God of all that is.

- Be unattached on an emotional level to the outcome of the request.

- The final stage is to know that you have contributed to the good of all, and thank all those unknown beings and people who have contributed to your desires.

When you do this, you are coming from your higher God self to the higher God self of the people concerned, who are creating the circumstances you want to influence for the good of all.

Once you have prepared yourself, it is easy. Your pure heart will do the rest.

Think of what you would like to create in the current situation. For example, you have heard that dolphins are being caught in the tuna nets. Sit down, and for five minutes a day see that this is not happening – a solution has been found by someone somewhere.

Eventually you will hear of the solution in the news and, being human, will not be sure if you helped at all or if it was just coincidence.

You have a saying that 'there are no coincidences'. It is something to keep in mind.

You can do this process for whatever your heart desires, with the caveat as described above that *it is for the good of all.*

For example, you could tackle efficient nondestructive fuel sources as well as your personal desires.

Send energy to the Earth and be grateful each day for what you have. When you are doing this, you are raising the energy of the Earth and helping your mother raise her energy and so creating fewer problems for her children.

Think of things you would like to practise on. It can be a wonderful and empowering experience.

# CHAPTER 4
## Newton´s Answers
## on Healing the Earth

I see Newton as really tall, with shades of metal.

Hello, Newton, it is good to meet you. I feel that you have the most radical ideas so far. I welcome them and look forward to hearing your ideas.

**Question:**

Please tell us about yourself, Newton.

**Answer:**

I am a multidimensional being that has ties to the Heart Nebula group. I look after planets; in a nutshell, you could say I am the gardener of planets. I hold their frequencies and orchestrate their spirits and keepers. The planets themselves grow and develop in their own way. They create life forms that embody their needs and resonate with their frequencies.

**Question:**

Did the human life forms on Earth come from the stars in the form of seeded cross-breeding of the original habitants?

**Answer:**

Yes and no. The Earth 'grew' its own life forms which prospered in their own way. The energy of the Earth and theirs was compatible. The Earth was agreeable to shifting its energy and accepting a newer and faster evolution process. Much like is happening now. So, at that time in history, the species were cross-bred, and with this the energy of the Earth also shifted.

You have a saying 'as above, so below'. There are many common sayings that are quite accurate. You, as modern men, have lost the conscious connection with the Earth. You still influence the Earth but are unaware of it. Similarly, the Earth influences you, and you are only aware of the inconvenience of droughts and the weather (a favourite).

**Question:**

What is it that you want to share with us?

**Answer:**

I want you to shift your vision of the Earth. Currently, the majority of you think of it as a large piece of rock. Yes, it has seas, and plants, and animals, and you – but you still see it as inanimate.

My intention is for more of you to see and feel the Earth as a very large being. A big Mama, if you will. The natives in many countries have done so for centuries. However, you in your modern times have often labelled this as primitive or superstitious. A brave few of you have taken on this concept of a planet that is in fact a being. A being that, as it turns out, is very complex.

Like all beings, plants and even rocks like to be appreciated and acknowledged. When you acknowledge something or somebody, you make it more solid – you enhance its creation. You are also showing gratitude to those things as well as to the divine who ultimately created them.

This is always a good thing to do. Think of your own life and the people who you resonate with. You happily do things for them simply to make them happy. What characteristics do they share? I am guessing when you write a list there will always be on the list something like:

They like me, appreciate me, support me, help me, etc. Along those lines.

So it is with other beings, inanimate objects, and your wonderful planet.

Do an experiment. Say there is a lid you cannot open and have tried many times, or a key that will not turn in a lock. Stop for a second and literally ask the lid or key to open the next time you try to open it. Of course, ask nicely. You will be surprised at how many times this works. You have respected the object by asking permission, and it usually agrees.

Then of course, it is a good idea to thank the object when you are done – to be grateful if only for a second.

**Question:**

What else would you like to share?

**Answer:**

I would like to get back to the topic of the Earth. One of the important emotions for the Earth – and also for you – is gratitude. The more you are grateful for something, the more it shows up in your life. The more you are disappointed with, say, your job, the more likely you are to lose it.

Think about the situations in your life when you were unhappy, but you would not acknowledge your thoughts as being negative. After a time, the situation or person disappeared; you usually find a reason to attribute this disappearance to. Then you walk about feeling like a victim because you lost something that in fact you were not happy with. Think of the times you have thought with true emotion and had your thoughts manifest.

When you think in the negative, you are also creating.

When you are grateful for something or someone, and demonstrate this in a word or thought, they tend to stay around. When you are grateful for your true friends, they are grateful for you. It is a bit of a cycle, which you can interrupt at will with your thoughts and words. This does not mean that every thought will manifest. It may be cancelled out by another thought or the power of other people's thoughts, or the highest good for all may take effect. However, when you keep reinforcing the same thought, it becomes more solid.

The Earth is like a very dear friend. It will help you all it can, but it too needs attention and support. It needs recognition and love, just as you and your friends do.

**Question:**

How can we help heal the Earth?

**Answer:**

Every morning, before you get up, lie in bed and think of the wonderful Earth below you. Thank it and send it love – to the heart of the Earth. It only takes seconds and means a lot to you and the Earth.

Among other things, it will give you a sense of balance and grounding.

There are support groups that are intent on helping the Earth deal with the amount of human refuse and needs – water, food, etc. Do not make fun of them. They are coming from a difficult place in a society that calls survival two cars, a large house, and utilities to match. It is not that these things are bad. It is just that they need to be constructed and powered in a way which is the least damaging for the Earth – rather than the most profitable for large groups.

Create a society in a way that uses your talents joyfully and in tune with the Earth.

Send messages of joy and love to the Earth. This you do by being joyful and loving. You are lightning rods that channel energy to the Earth. There is much incentive to channel happy, grateful, and trusting energy to the Earth, for both you and the Earth.

Practise some of the communication techniques with frequency and visualisations that help the Earth.

Remember the Sun in the morning; be grateful that the Sun is the father of your world, working at evaporating water and keeping you warm. Whether you see it or not during the day, it is there shining on your Earth. It would be a cold world indeed if the sun did not shine on you.

In summary:

- Recognise the Earth as a being.

- Acknowledge what she does for you.

- Be grateful for all you have and what she has given you.

- In the same way you can recognise the Sun – the life-giving force of the Yang to the Earth's Yin.

- Band together to encourage politicians and companies to create Earth-friendly products on a physical level.

- Use your thoughts and abilities to manifest on the frequency level, in order to shift the world into a more viable planet for the 7.8 billon plus people on the Earth.

**Question:**

Is there anything else you would like to communicate?

**Answer:**

Thank you for your time and effort in writing this book on our behalf, from all of us. As you say, 'we wish you the best' in love from the Heart Nebula.

# CHAPTER 5

# Beyond the Earth Questions

In this section, I have been guided to go beyond the conversations thus far. It is an area of interest for some and not for others. I myself have not really dealt in this arena till now. I have actively avoided it, except for my fascination with Star Trek and some sci-fi.

There seem to be so many levels on our *simple* Earth:

The physical, as in humans and animals;

The inanimate, as in rocks, crystals, earth, and trees;

The spirits yet to depart;

The guides we all have;

The angels that help when needed;

The creator of all that is.

These are the things I have been comfortable with and aware of.

Now I would like to add one more large group:

Visitors from the rest of the Universe.

There are billions of planets that are similar to our own. Since we have been created as a mixture of various DNA, we resemble what others would call UFOs or extra-terrestrials. Over the years, there have been many sightings of humanoid-type extra-terrestrials.

**My question to Angie is:**

How do these visitors from the stars affect us?

**Answer:**

On Earth there are many variations of the same species. You do not interact with them all or even know of them all. You have your world, so to speak, and basically you have your soul purpose ready at hand in your world. There is no need for most of you to seek elsewhere, unless it is a calling from your soul and it makes you happy. It is not necessary for you to investigate the other forms of existence in and out of your world.

There is no need for you to know everything or experience everything in this lifetime. You have many lifetimes and many forms that you will inhabit and experience. At this point, the person you are now in the form you are in now is here to learn under these conditions.

Never feel sorry for anyone – each of you is doing what you need to do at the time. You can have compassion and support, but judging someone else's life and feeling sorry for them takes away their power of choice and the lessons they want to learn. As the saying goes, 'Don't judge someone until you've walked a mile in their shoes.'

That being said, some of you are in fact programmed to connect with Extra-terrestrials and work with them. You will know who you are by the interest and fascination you derive from learning about them.

**Question:**

Will extra-terrestrials help the Earth at this shifting time?

**Answer:**

The label extra-terrestrials is painted with a very large brush. Some are here to help; some are here to plunder. There are many advantages to be had in a time of confusion. Many have been here and are incorporated into our societies. They continue to influence the Earth and its population. They are still incorporated in our societies but are becoming weaker in their influence as the Earth itself is shifting frequency, those with lower vibrations are not as comfortable here or as willing to submit to the changes. In this case, they will be absorbed or leave.

But getting back to the point at hand, some of these extra-terrestrials will enjoy the new frequencies and support the Earth. Like everything, there is no real good or bad. There are humans who are constructive, and those who can be destructive – and so it is with the extra-terrestrials. When you come across these energies, look at who or what they are through the filter of your intuition, and not through fear or judgement. Hearsay has been used to manipulate large numbers of people – it is something to be wary of. Go by how your heart feels. The more you come from love and higher frequencies, the clearer will be your intuition. The more you use it, the stronger it will be.

The extra-terrestrials here to help the Earth are in the process of doing so. It is not something that you would normally focus on or tune into unless it is in your soul purpose.

Those from the Pleiades, Sirius, and Andromeda Galaxy are supporting and helping you at this time. The planets themselves are affecting your shift.

**My question to Newton is:**

How do extra-terrestrials compare with our guides and angels?

**Answer:**

They really do not. It is like comparing eggs and oranges. They can be generally considered another species of physical matter. Much like you have variations of human groups on this planet. Extraterrestrials are another variation of physical form from another planet or planets.

They have different levels of advancement, depending on the group. They can help you in physical ways and generally communicate telepathically. The assumption being that if they came to the Earth, they are advanced in many levels, including telepathy.

Your guides and angels are for your support and help when you ask for it. They have no agenda other than to help you. Extra-terrestrials may be benevolent and helpful depending on the frequency they are – they will also have their group interests and responsibilities in mind.

Your guides and angels consider your requests and needs to be the main focus for them. Your guides and angels are usually of a higher frequency and do not incorporate in bodies. This gives them more freedom and a higher perspective, in the sense that there is less attachment to the physical.

# CHAPTER 6

## Questions on Changing Times for George

**Question:**

Are there beings dwelling within the Earth?

**Answer:**

Yes, there are beings dwelling within the Earth.

**Question:**

Will they be affected by the shift?

**Answer:**

Yes. However, in general they are more prepared for the changes. They are closer to the heartbeat of the Earth. They have been shifting and changing in preparation. You may even see some on the surface of the Earth.

**Question:**

What is the best way for us to move forward at this time?

**Answer:**

First and foremost is to have faith that you and your family will be looked after. Know that if it rains, the sun will soon shine on you.

Ask to be in the right place for you at the right time – and trust it to be so. Remember – *ask and you shall receive.*

Next, think of what it is you truly want. What is your soul calling for, while your body calls for survival?

Who do you want to help?

What do you want to experience?

These questions do not take much time to ask. Patiently wait for the answers to come to you. They will come. Again, have faith in those guides and angels supporting you. You are not alone. If nothing else, take a moment to appreciate the nature that you can see near you: a plant, a tree. Or if not available, imagine your feet touching the Earth and gaining support and energy from it.

See your feet grow roots to nourish you from the Earth below the cement.

You are an infinite being experiencing this Earth and time. You chose to be here on this Earth – take ownership of your infinite spiritual strength and support.

Observe and be thankful for each morsel of kindness given to you. Like a garden watered, it grows and flourishes.

Let go of what others believe and what you think they should believe. Remember, God gave you free will here. Give the same gift to others without the chains of your judgement. You know neither what they have been through in other lives nor what their goals are in this experience. Their connection to you is also special and may simply be a mirror of your hidden wounds.

If you are reading this, one of your goals is to support the Earth and all on her. There are many ways to do this. You may want to join groups, or come from a more isolated individual place. This can be a simple thing. Just add joy and love to your life. Make it a focus where you can and when you can. The more you focus on something and take action, the more of it you have, and the easier it becomes.

This will transmit joy to the Earth and shift those around you.

**Question:**

How can you balance yourself in the face of antagonism on these subjects from those you care about?

**Answer:**

Remember – you are not a victim. You are strong in love and support from all levels.

If others do not approve of your beliefs and behaviour, they are struggling with the news feeds and many conflicting external and internal beliefs and emotions.

These people are also a reflection of your own inner turmoil. The clearer and more loving you are, the less problems you will have with them. Your shift will be their shift. If nothing else, when you visualise harmonious relationships surrounding you, they will appear – they may be the same people you were uncomfortable with before, or they may be new people appearing in your life.

Their triggers do not have to be your triggers, unless the cords between you include these triggers.

A helpful exercise could be the following:

Imagine a pair of scissors cutting the cords of triggers that bind you in negative emotions. Do this as many times as you need to.

Then heal the cords and seal them with violet light – or whatever light comes to mind.

All this can be done while talking to or listening to them, as well as at a separate time and place from them.

Your intention is always the key. If you are not strong at the time, defer the exercise till you feel stronger. Or just keep doing it till you are stronger!

In the meantime, bathe yourself in light. Again, whatever colour comes to mind – your soul knows what it is doing. It will be whatever colour you need when you need it, in alignment with your intentions.

If you are having trouble knowing what colour to use, try golden or blue.

These may seem like simple visualisations – and they are. It does not have to be complicated. It is based on love and three other things:

1. Intention – to help yourself and others

2. Letting go – of judgement of others

3. Forgiveness – of yourself and others for being human at this time of growth and learning.

A change can occur in the blink of an eye. Relationships can shift so fast it is hard to believe it is real. Then you need to keep up the visualisations as the new reality sinks into your mind and being. Anchor your new relationship rather than going back in your mind to compare what it used to be like. Stay in your intention for your relationships.

The visualisations do not have to be perfect – they will grow, as most things do with practice.

The basis is love – coming from the heart and hence the heart of God.

**Question:**

What can we do to help our bodies at this time?

**Answer:**

Drink tea and relax!

Your bodies, as well as your emotions and soul, are undergoing rapid shifts.

1.  The more you support your soul purpose, spirit, and feel emotions of joy, the less energy your body will need to fight stress and confusion. The more time it will have to heal and grow in strength.

2.  Your body needs to move – it is built that way. When there is no movement in the body, it atrophies. The muscles and lymph cannot function properly. Your heart is a muscle, so it too needs movement in your life to clear the cells of waste and debris.

3.  Unless you have movement and some form of exercise, your body – which was also built to regenerate – will not be able to do so effectively. The cells become full of waste and diseases take over. The garbage in your body has not been fully removed.

4.  Your body uses the clean-up crew/system, which is composed of organisms to break down the decaying body cells. The crew is made up of bacteria, viruses, fungus, and parasites, whose job it is to recycle your body back to the Earth. They start to grow in number to get rid of the dead wood in your body.

So, in times of stress:

- Yes, rest.

- Move more and exercise even by dancing around the room for a few minutes. Or shaking your body to release tension and get the meridians and fluids moving. There is no set way to shake, so it really is intuitive and fun.

- Eat lightly – as is always said, lots of alkalizing vegetables as fresh as you can get them. Water to flush out the accumulated waste in your cells.

- Avoid drugs of any kind on a regular basis. Legal and illegal. They are a distraction and dull your spirit. They encourage the entrance into your aura of other forms of parasites, which prey on the weak. This can result in anger, fights, fear, and confusion. If you suspect something of the sort, remember to declare that they do not have permission to be in your energy field. For the good of all, send them away.

- The best drug is to breathe in coloured light deeply, whatever colour you need at the time. A few breaths will clear the fog that has enveloped you.

- The sun is a wonderful relaxant and healer. If there is no sun, breathe in the memory of the warmth and relaxation.

The more you exercise in some form, sleep well, eat well, and avoid drugs, the healthier you will be and the stronger your body will be to resist illness.

One more point. On the whole you will not need as much food as you have been eating.

See Lydia's up-and-coming book *A Joyfull Relationship with Your Body and Soul* for more detailed discussion of your body and the new relationship you will have with it.

God bless you all. I send my love to carry you on your journey forward with the Mother Earth.

# Parting Words

You can be strong. You can do these visualisations and others that come to you to make a difference to the shifting Earth and those on her.

You are powerful. You are part of God and creation. Ask for support and you will receive it. Have faith in yourself and the process. All IS well.

# From the Author

Thank you for reading this book. I wish you and your family and friends love and success in your soul path and in the physical world. I hope you enjoyed this book and my angels' guidance as much as I enjoyed writing it.

I truly appreciate any reviews you can give for this book – even if only a sentence.

I can be contacted at:

My website – https://LydiaAnneMitchell.com

Facebook : www.facebook.com/lydia.mitchell.9022/

Twitter: twitter.com/LydiaAnneMitch1

Instagram: LydiaAnneMitchell (@lydiaannemitchell)

LinkedIn: Lydia Anne Mitchell

My first book, for those awakening to their spiritual journey, *Spiritual Reality: Transforming the Ordinary into the Extraordinary*, can be purchased at the following links:

balboapress.com/en/bookstore/bookdetails/761701-Spiritual-Reality

https://amzn.to/3wYReri

**Up-and-coming books by Lydia Anne Mitchell, Ph.D.**

*Joy in Your Integrated Soul*

*A Joyfull Relationship with Your Body and Soul*

*Your Soul Relationship with All Living Things*

*Your Soul Relationship with Inanimate Matter*

*You Can Create a New World*